THE 40 DAY FEAST FOR YOUR SOUL

TEN SPIRITUAL DISHES TO REFRESH YOUR LIFE

PETE CHAPMAN

WESTBOW
PRESS®
A DIVISION OF THOMAS NELSON
& ZONDERVAN

WestBow Press books may be ordered through booksellers or by contacting:

WestBow Press
A Division of Thomas Nelson & Zondervan
1663 Liberty Drive
Bloomington, IN 47403
www.westbowpress.com
1 (866) 928-1240

ISBN: 978-1-9736-1323-7 (sc)
ISBN: 978-1-9736-1324-4 (e)

Library of Congress Control Number: 2018904661

Print information available on the last page.

WestBow Press rev. date: 05/10/2018

Contents

Preface

Welcome to the *Forty-Day Feast for Your Soul*. This book will help you to connect with yourself and the people around you in ways you may never have imagined were possible. It will also open your eyes to see new spiritual possibilities and purpose for your life.

Our society places such emphasis on body transformation, beauty makeovers, and spiritual discovery, yet little is written about nurturing our own souls. For thousands of years, religious people practised spiritual disciplines to stay centered and close to God. The forty-day feast makes that ancient wisdom accessible today using simple exercises based on biblical principles.

Feasting your soul is not just about achieving greater things for your own life. By caring for your soul, you will be an inspiration to others as well.

> *For while bodily training is of some value, godliness*
> *is of value in every way, as it holds promise for*
> *the present life and also for the life to come.*
> —1 Timothy 4:8 (KJV)

This is the first of many verses quoted from the Bible. The Bible is divided into books, chapters and verses, and these are shown after each verse so you can look them up for yourself. For example, this verse was from the book of 1 Timothy (there are two books written by Timothy) chapter 4 verse 8.

Everyone reading this book brings their own unique background. For many, it will be your first encounter with true soul food, and a nibble each day will satisfy you. For others, you've already dined on some of these dishes so often that you know them by heart. They have become like old friends, regular companions, and part of your daily routine.

These forty days are just the start. The principles that underpin each dish never grow old, and I hope you are inspired to build them into your everyday life. There is still so much just waiting for you to discover.

I pray that this is the start of an incredibly rewarding journey which will continue for the rest of your life.

Pete Chapman
Sydney, February 2018

Acknowledgments

For Claire, my amazing wife and soul mate.
Your inspiration and tireless support made this book possible.
Thank you for everything.

Introduction

What Is Soul Food?

In this book, you will be feasting on things that are great for your soul. The dishes are based on ten simple principles that have been practised through the ages. When these become daily or weekly habits, they continually nourish your soul and build up your strength both inside and out. Good soul food has the power to free you from toxic mind-sets, reconnect broken relationships, create new friendships, and help you to discover a deeper purpose in life. As you invigorate your own soul, the effects overflow into the lives of others, inspiring those around you and changing the atmosphere in your world.

Soul food describes the things that affect your mind, your will, and your emotions. Some things are good for your soul, like reading great books or being generous. And some things are junk, like bad movies or holding on to bitter feelings. If you live on junk, you will eventually get sick and need help.

The wonderful thing about soul food is that you can feast without getting fat. A common mistake is trying to feed soul hunger with food for your physical body. It's just not meant to be that way, and our body lets us know. But when we feed on soul food, there is no guilt, and there are no bad side effects. Instead of getting fat and bloated, we continue to grow into better people. The more we feast, the more benefits overflow into our lives and the lives around us.

These forty days are just a launching point. Every dish has its own rich history. People have devoted lifetimes to mastering each of them.

At the end of forty days, look back and see how you have changed. Decide which dishes you want to continue and build them into your daily routine. Tell your friends about your feast and encourage them to try it as well.

Are you ready for a feast? Then let's get started!

The Next Forty Days

Why does this feast go for forty days? Numbers had special significance to ancient writers, partly because their alphabet was also their number system. Words and numbers interlink and significant numbers were associated with themes in a system called gematria.

In the case of the number forty, the association is new beginnings. Noah's new beginning came after forty days and nights of rain. The Israelites finally reached their promised land after wandering for forty years in the Sinai Desert. Jesus began his ministry after forty days alone in the desert.

Another important number is five, which is associated with grace or undeserved kindness. As an example, many of the measurements in the plans for the tabernacle in Exodus 26, an important symbol of grace, are five or multiples of five.

Forty days just happens to comprise five weeks and five days. That's a double serving of grace—the perfect accompaniment to any new beginning!

For forty days, you will feast on ten dishes that are described in more detail on the following pages. Some dishes can be enjoyed every day, and others are just once per week.

The first five dishes focus on your personal thoughts and attitudes.

- forty times of thankfulness
- forty prayers for others
- forty hours of fasting
- forty verses to know
- forty chapters to read

The second five dishes focus on how you engage with people around you.

- forty messages of encouragement
- forty hours of generosity
- forty acts of forgiveness
- forty faces of kindness
- forty hours of rest

To help structure the days and weeks of your feast, I have arranged the dishes into a menu. Of course, you don't have to eat everything on the menu. Take as much or as little as you like from each dish. The most valuable thing to do during your feast is to come back to the menu regularly each day and stay filled.

Daily Menu

Appetizers

Appetizers are a great way to start your day. The psalmist used to get up before dawn to consume dishes like these. You will probably need about half an hour to get through them and digest them properly.

Times of Thankfulness

Start your daily feast by spending time thinking of things that make you thankful. It could be health, family, friends, finances, or just having a roof over your head today. This dish is most important when it's hardest to do. There is a spiritual principle that thankfulness opens the gates to the presence of God.

In every thing give thanks: for this is the will of God in Christ Jesus concerning you.
—1 Thessalonians 5:18 (KJV)

Prayers for Others

Whether you believe in it or not, prayer is powerful and effective. Not only can it unlock spiritual power, but it also releases compassion toward other people in your own soul.

Be alert and always keep on praying for all the Lord's people.
—Ephesians 6:18 (NIV)

Acts of Forgiveness

This is a hugely important part of your feast and general well-being. Let go of any grudge and forgive anyone who has hurt you. Seek forgiveness from anyone you have hurt. Start with the first person who comes to mind and experience the incredible freedom that comes with forgiveness.

Therefore, if you are offering your gift at the altar and there remember that your brother or sister has something against you, leave your gift there in front of the altar.
First go and be reconciled to that person;
then come and offer your gift.
—Matthew 5:23–24 (NIV)

Main Dishes

Main dishes should be consumed throughout
the day or incorporated into your routine.

Chapters to Read

I've listed a chapter from scripture for each day in the
forty-day calendar, or you can choose your own reading
plan if you prefer. Start reading the chapter. If something
stands out, then stop and linger there. Take time to
allow any verses that spark your attention to soak into
your soul and your being. Meditate on the words.

If you have time, also read the proverb that
corresponds to the day of the month. For example,
on the tenth day of the month, read Proverbs 10.

Your word is a lamp to my feet and a light to my path.
—Psalm 119:105 (ESV)

Hours of Generosity

Find some way to be generous to another person, even if he
or she doesn't know it comes from you. The spiritual principle
behind this dish is to give, and it shall be given to you[1].

For God loves a cheerful giver ...
You will be enriched in every way to be generous
on every occasion, and your giving through
us will produce thanksgiving to God.
—2 Corinthians 9:7, 11 (BSB)

---

[1] Luke 6:38

Messages of Encouragement

Speak words of life and encouragement into the people around you. Know how to speak a word in season, as described in Proverbs 15:23.

Continually encourage one another every day, as long as it is called "Today."
—Hebrews 3:13 (AB)

Faces of Kindness

Look at the people around you and smile. Put on a cheerful disposition by having a happy face. You have nothing to lose and everything to gain.

A cheerful disposition is good for your health.
—Proverbs 17:22 (MSG)

Desserts

Dessert is the perfect ending as you finish your day.

Verses to Know

Review the memory verse from yesterday and memorize today's verse listed in the forty-day calendar. The Bible describes itself as alive and active, judging the thoughts and attitudes of the heart[2]. Memorizing verses is one of the most powerful things you can do for your soul. You are literally feasting on the living Word.

> *Guard my teaching as the apple of your eye.*
> *Bind them on your fingers.*
> *Write them on the tablet of your heart.*
> —Proverbs 7:2–3 (WEB)

Weekly Specials

Think about which days will work best for these weekly dishes. You will probably have to rearrange your diary to accommodate them. Diaries (and wallets) let you know where your priorities lie. Some changes are a healthy sign that your soul is getting more attention.

---

[2] Hebrews 4:12

Hours of Rest

Take a day to rest from things that stress you
out and focus on the relationships that matter
most. There's more to life than working, and
rest is one of the Ten Commandments.

For six days work may be done,
but the seventh day shall be a holy day for you,
a Sabbath of complete rest to the Lord.
—Exodus 35:2 (AB)

Hours of Fasting

Give your stomach a break, and your soul
will thank you. Fasting is an ancient spiritual
discipline with many wonderful benefits.

Blessed are you who hunger now,
For you shall be filled.
—Luke 6:21 (NKJV)

Ten Dishes

The daily menu and weekly specials introduced ten dishes to enjoy during your feast. In this section each dish is described in detail, with an explanation of how to consume it and what impact it can have on your life.

Forty Times of Thankfulness

Enter into his gates with thanksgiving,
and into his courts with praise:
be thankful unto him, and bless his name.
—Psalm 100:4 (KJV)

Activity

Make time each day to say thank you. This is a great way to start your day.

Motivation

Thankfulness opens the gates of heaven in our lives.

Method

Say thank you for everything that comes to mind. If you're drawing a blank, then *thank you* on its own is enough. This activity is most effective when you speak thanks out loud and not just in your head.

Related Scriptures

In every thing give thanks: for this is the will
of God in Christ Jesus concerning you.
—1 Thessalonians 5:18 (KJV)

Give thanks to the Lord, for he is good; his love endures forever.
—Psalm 107:1 (NIV)

And whatever you do, in word or deed, do everything in the name
of the Lord Jesus, giving thanks to God the Father through him.
—Colossians 3:17 (ESV)

Forty Prayers for Others

Do not be anxious about anything,
but in every situation, by prayer and petition,
with thanksgiving, present your requests to God.
—Philippians 4:6 (NIV)

Activity

Pray for someone you know every day.

Motivation

Charles Spurgeon characterized prayer perfectly by explaining that "prayer is the slender nerve that moves the muscle of omnipotence." God can do anything but chooses to do it when we pray.

Method

Pray for someone you know. Pray for success or a breakthrough in some area of their life. Pray for healing if they are unwell. Make time to think about their circumstances, wait for something specific to come to mind, and then pray for that.

Keep notes about your prayers and look back from time to time to see them making a difference.

Related Scriptures

"If you believe,
you will receive whatever you ask for in prayer."
—Matthew 21:22 (NIV)

The prayer of a righteous person is powerful and effective.
—James 5:16 (NIV)

Until now you have not asked for anything in my name.
Ask and you will receive, and your joy will be complete.
—John 16:24 (NIV)

Devote yourselves to prayer with an alert
mind and a thankful heart.
—Colossians 4:2 (NLT)

Likewise the Spirit helps us in our weakness.
For we do not know what to pray for as we ought,
but the Spirit himself intercedes for us with
groanings too deep for words.
—Romans 8:26 (ESV)

Forty Hours of Fasting

Blessed are you who hunger now, for you shall be filled.
—Luke 6:21 (NKJV)

Activity

Abstain from some or all food for at least eight hours each week. You should check with your doctor before making any significant changes to diet, particularly if you are pregnant or suffering from any kind of medical condition.

Motivation

Divert energy from your body to your soul. Activate your self-control and increase your appreciation for food.

Method

Before you start the fast, decide the type of fast you will do and when you will do it.

A total fast means you don't eat or drink anything except water. A partial fast means stopping only certain foods or drinks, such as coffee, chocolate, animal products, anything with sugar, or solid foods.

Some people start their fast after dinner when the sun goes down and finish twenty-four hours later, missing breakfast and lunch. Others fast for a calendar day, missing breakfast, lunch, and dinner.

Don't stop drinking water. Healthy people can go without food for a day, but our bodies need plenty of water every day.

Related Scriptures

No discipline seems enjoyable at the time, but painful.
Later on, however, it yields a peaceful harvest of
righteousness to those who have been trained by it.
—Hebrews 12:11 (BSB)

"Yet even now," declares the LORD,
"return to me with all your heart, with fasting,
with weeping, and with mourning."
—Joel 2:12 (ESV)

I proclaimed a fast, so that we might humble ourselves
before our God and ask him for a safe journey for
us and our children, with all our possessions.
—Ezra 8:21 (NIV)

Forty Verses to Know

When I discovered your words, I devoured them.
They are my joy and my heart's delight.
—Jeremiah 15:16 (NLT)

Activity

Work to memorize verses from the Bible every day.

Motivation

The verses you memorize create solid foundations for your future and shelter for the inevitable storms[3].

Method

In the forty-day calendar, I have selected verses for each day that relate to the ten dishes. When you memorize a verse, try to get the exact words and remember the reference as well. If it is too hard to memorize the whole verse, then focus on getting the reference right so you can find it when needed.

Memory is like a muscle that improves with practice, so the forty-day calendar starts with shorter verses. Repetition is the key.

At the start of the day, read the verse over until you can repeat it without looking. Then repeat regularly throughout the rest of the day to make sure it sticks. Some tricky verses can take a while to learn, but once you've remembered them, they will be with you for life.

---

[3] Psalm 119:114

Related Scriptures

"Then you will know the truth, and the truth will set you free."
—John 8:32 (NIV)

All Scripture is God-breathed and is useful
for teaching, rebuking, correcting and training in righteousness.
—2 Timothy 3:16 (NIV)

So shall my word be that goes out from my mouth;
it shall not return to me empty, but it shall
accomplish that which I purpose,
and shall succeed in the thing for which I sent it.
—Isaiah 55:11 (ESV)

Your word is a lamp to guide my feet and a light for my path.
—Psalm 119:105 (NLT)

Forty Chapters to Read

Jesus answered, "It is written:
'People do not live on bread alone, but on every word
that comes from the mouth of God.'"
—Matthew 4:4 (NIV)

Activity

Read a complete passage from the Bible every day.

Motivation

Reading scripture sustains your spirit and lights your way.

Method

In the forty-day calendar, I've listed a Bible chapter to read every day. These scriptures have inspired people for hundreds of years.

You will need a Bible for this dish. Free Bible apps are available online and most bookstores sell Bibles. Over the years different groups have translated the original Greek and Hebrew scrolls into English which is why there are different Bible versions. The broad meanings are the same, but writing style can vary a lot! Choose a version that you enjoy reading. In this book I've drawn from many different versions, shown in brackets after each verse and detailed in the opening pages.

Another great habit is to read a daily chapter from Proverbs. You could do this in addition to the chapter I've listed. There are thirty-one chapters in Proverbs, one for each day of the month. For example, on July 4, you could read Proverbs 4.

The selection of chapters is based on how frequently they appear in internet searches. These chapters aren't "better" than the rest of the Bible but they do tend to be better known.

Related Scriptures

The grass withers, the flower fades,
But the word of our God stands forever.
—Isaiah 40:8 (NASB)

For the word of God is living and active,
sharper than any two-edged sword,
piercing to the division of soul and of
spirit, of joints and of marrow,
and discerning the thoughts and intentions of the heart.
—Hebrews 4:12 (ESV)

In the beginning was the Word,
and the Word was with God,
and the Word was God.
—John 1:1 (KJV)

Forty Messages of Encouragement

Therefore encourage one another and build one another up,
just as you are doing.
—1 Thessalonians 5:11 (ESV)

Activity

Be an encourager.

Motivation

Make someone's world a little better every day.

Method

Impact someone positively each day by encouraging them with
a compliment, a note, or a token of appreciation.

Related Scriptures

Death and life are in the power of the tongue,
and those who love it will eat its fruits.
—Proverbs 18:21 (ESV)

There is one who speaks rashly, like a piercing sword;
but the tongue of the wise brings healing.
—Proverbs 12:18 (HOL)

A soothing tongue is a tree of life,
But perversion in it crushes the spirit.
—Proverbs 15:4 (NASB)

Forty Hours of Generosity

One person gives freely, yet gains more;
another withholds what is right, only to become poor.
—Proverbs 11:24 (HOL)

Activity

Give away the equivalent of one hour per day.

Motivation

Fight materialism and greed with generosity.

Method

Give the equivalent of forty hours of wages in money, time, or possessions during your forty-day feast. If possible, give secretly to avoid awkwardness and to keep your motives true.

In giving generously, don't forget another principle of wise stewardship:

Owe no one anything, except to love each other,
for the one who loves another has fulfilled the law.
—Romans 13:8 (ESV)

You will give in different ways at different times of your life. For some, giving the equivalent of an hour each day sounds like a lot. On the other hand, when we were raising small children, an hour of not giving for Claire seemed rare! Here are some suggestions of things you could give to someone else:

- housework

- yardwork

- handyman jobs

- cleaning windows

- gardening

- shopping

- running errands

- doing a chore that someone else normally does

- babysitting

- making and delivering a meal

- for tradesmen and professionals, doing a job for free

Related Scriptures

*Each one must give as he has decided in his heart, not reluctantly
or under compulsion, for God loves a cheerful giver.*
—2 Corinthians 9:7 (ESV)

*But when you give to someone in need,
don't let your left hand know what your right hand is doing.*
—Matthew 6:3 (NLT)

*Give, and it will be given to you.
A good measure, pressed down, shaken together,
and running over will be poured into your lap.
For with the measure you use, it will be measured back to you.*
—Luke 6:38 (BSB)

You will be made enriched in every way so that
you can be generous on every occasion,
and through us your generosity will result in thanksgiving to God.
—2 Corinthians 9:11 (NIV)

In the midst of a very severe trial, their overflowing joy
and their extreme poverty welled up in rich generosity.
—2 Corinthians 8:2 (NIV)

Forty Acts of Forgiveness

For if you forgive other people when they sin against you,
your heavenly Father will also forgive you.
—Matthew 6:14 (NIV)

Activity

Forgive someone each day or ask for forgiveness where you have
done wrong.

Motivation

Forgiveness sets you free to embrace a better future. "Resentment
is like drinking a poison and then waiting for the other person
to die.[4]" Unforgiveness and bitterness holds you back from a
better future.

Method

Perform an act of forgiveness. Forgiveness may be given or
received.

You can apologize and ask forgiveness from someone you've hurt.

Or you can offer forgiveness to someone who has hurt you.

It's okay if you need to repeat the same act of forgiveness over
many days while your emotions catch up with your words.

---

[4] Actress Carrie Fisher paraphrasing The Sermon on the Mount (1938) by
Emmet Fox who wrote "You will hardly have any doubt as to who will receive
the benefit of the poison."

Even when your anger or resentment are totally justified, or if the other person has passed away, whatever the situation forgiveness is your key to being able to move on.

It may help to do something tangible, like writing out the offense and then destroying the pages forever.

Ultimately, we have all fallen short and hurt other people by doing things that are wrong, on purpose and by accident. The greatest act of forgiveness came from God Himself when he sent Jesus Christ to die in our place. Everyone is invited to receive His forgiveness. You can read more about being completely forgiven in the final chapter.

Related Scriptures

> *Bear with each other and forgive any complaint you may have against one another. Forgive as the Lord forgave you.*
> —Colossians 3:13 (BSB)

> *For all have sinned and fall short of the glory of God.*
> —Romans 3:23 (ESV)

> *For if you forgive other people when they sin against you, your heavenly Father will also forgive you.*
> —Matthew 6:14 (NIV)

> *Peter replied, "Repent and be baptized, every one of you, in the name of Jesus Christ for the forgiveness of your sins, and you will receive the gift of the Holy Spirit."*
> —Acts 2:38 (BSB)

Forty Faces of Kindness

A joyful heart makes a cheerful face,
but when the heart is sad, the spirit is broken.
—Proverbs 15:13 (NASB)

Activity

Smile at someone.

Motivation

A happy heart makes the face cheerful.

Method

Just smile. Think about things that make you feel happy and let the world know with a smile on your face.

Related Scriptures

The light of the eyes rejoices the heart,
and good news refreshes the bones.
—Proverbs 15:30 (ESV)

So I commend the enjoyment of life,
because there is nothing better for people under the sun
than to eat and drink and be glad.
Then joy will accompany them in their toil
all the days of the life God has given them under the sun.
—Ecclesiastes 8:15 (NIV)

*Now may the God of hope fill you with all joy and
peace as you believe in Him, so that you may overflow
with hope by the power of the Holy Spirit.*
—Romans 15:13 (BSB)

*But the fruit of the Spirit is
love, joy, peace, patience, kindness, goodness,
faithfulness, gentleness, self-control;
against such things there is no law.*
—Galatians 5:22–23 (NASB)

Forty Hours of Rest

For six days work may be done, but the seventh
day shall be a holy day for you,
a Sabbath of complete rest to the Lord.
—Exodus 35:2 (AMP)

Activity

Rest from work-related activities for one day each week.

Motivation

Make space for more important things in life.

Method

Choose one day each week and be disciplined about resting from your usual weekly chores. Spend the time with family and friends or relaxing and enjoying hobbies. Some people switch off their screens for the day or eat preprepared meals using disposable plates to avoid the work of washing up.

Related Scriptures

Come to me, all you who are weary and burdened,
and I will give you rest.
—Matthew 11:28 (NIV)

Whoever dwells in the shelter of the Most High
will rest in the shadow of the Almighty.
—Psalm 91:1 (NIV)

There remains, then, a Sabbath rest for the people of God;
for anyone who enters God's rest also rests from their works,
just as God did from his.
—Hebrews 4:9–10 (ESV)

One person considers one day more sacred than
another; another considers every day alike.
Each of them should be fully convinced in their own mind.
—Romans 14:5 (NIV)

Forty-Day Calendar

Here is the daily program for your forty day feast.

Each day lists all ten dishes from the menu, with a specific verse to know and a chapter to read. There is also a space for notes so that you can keep track of your progress and capture new thoughts and insights as you enjoy each dish in your feast.

Like any menu, you don't have to eat everything that's on it. Choose the dishes that your soul craves the most. You can always come back again later and feast some more.

Try to taste at least one thing from the menu every day during the forty days. Consistently dipping in is more effective than a burst of enthusiasm that you can't sustain.

Day 1

Time of Thankfulness	
Prayer for Others	
Act of Forgiveness	
Chapter to Read	Psalm 1
Hour of Generosity	
Message of Encouragement	
Face of Kindness	
Verse to Know	*Your word is a lamp to my feet and a light to my path.* —Psalm 119:105 (ESV)
Resting Day?	
Fasting Day?	

Day 2

Time of Thankfulness	
Prayer for Others	
Act of Forgiveness	
Chapter to Read	Genesis 1
Hour of Generosity	
Message of Encouragement	
Face of Kindness	
Verse to Know	*For all have sinned and fall short of the glory of God.* —Romans 3:23 (ESV)
Resting Day?	
Fasting Day?	

Day 3

Time of Thankfulness	
Prayer for Others	
Act of Forgiveness	
Chapter to Read	Psalm 15
Hour of Generosity	
Message of Encouragement	
Face of Kindness	
Verse to Know	*Blessed are you who hunger now, For you shall be filled.* —Luke 6:21 (NKJV)
Resting Day?	
Fasting Day?	

Day 4

Time of Thankfulness	
Prayer for Others	
Act of Forgiveness	
Chapter to Read	1 Corinthians 13
Hour of Generosity	
Message of Encouragement	
Face of Kindness	
Verse to Know	*"If you believe, you will receive whatever you ask for in prayer."* —Matthew 21:22 (NIV)
Resting Day?	
Fasting Day?	

Day 5

Time of Thankfulness	
Prayer for Others	
Act of Forgiveness	
Chapter to Read	Psalm 16
Hour of Generosity	
Message of Encouragement	
Face of Kindness	
Verse to Know	*Heaven and earth will pass away, but my words will never pass away.* —Matthew 24:35 (NIV)
Resting Day?	
Fasting Day?	

Day 6

Time of Thankfulness	
Prayer for Others	
Act of Forgiveness	
Chapter to Read	Hebrews 13
Hour of Generosity	
Message of Encouragement	
Face of Kindness	
Verse to Know	*The light of the eyes rejoices the heart.* —Proverbs 15:30 (KJV)
Resting Day?	
Fasting Day?	

Day 7

Time of Thankfulness	
Prayer for Others	
Act of Forgiveness	
Chapter to Read	Psalm 23
Hour of Generosity	
Message of Encouragement	
Face of Kindness	
Verse to Know	*A soothing tongue is a tree of life, But perversion in it crushes the spirit.* —Proverbs 15:4 (NASB)
Resting Day?	
Fasting Day?	

Day 8

Time of Thankfulness	
Prayer for Others	
Act of Forgiveness	
Chapter to Read	Matthew 5
Hour of Generosity	
Message of Encouragement	
Face of Kindness	
Verse to Know	*But when you give to someone in need, don't let your left hand know what your right hand is doing.* —Matthew 6:3 (NLT)
Resting Day?	
Fasting Day?	

Day 9

Time of Thankfulness	
Prayer for Others	
Act of Forgiveness	
Chapter to Read	Psalm 34
Hour of Generosity	
Message of Encouragement	
Face of Kindness	
Verse to Know	*Devote yourselves to prayer with an alert mind and a thankful heart.* —Colossians 4:2 (NLT)
Resting Day?	
Fasting Day?	

Day 10

Time of Thankfulness	
Prayer for Others	
Act of Forgiveness	
Chapter to Read	Matthew 6
Hour of Generosity	
Message of Encouragement	
Face of Kindness	
Verse to Know	*The grass withers, the flower fades, But the word of our God stands forever.* —Isaiah 40:8 (NASB)
Resting Day?	
Fasting Day?	

Day 11

Time of Thankfulness	
Prayer for Others	
Act of Forgiveness	
Chapter to Read	Psalm 37
Hour of Generosity	
Message of Encouragement	
Face of Kindness	
Verse to Know	*Death and life are in the power of the tongue, and those who love it will eat its fruits.* —Proverbs 18:21 (ESV)
Resting Day?	
Fasting Day?	

Day 12

Time of Thankfulness	
Prayer for Others	
Act of Forgiveness	
Chapter to Read	Matthew 7
Hour of Generosity	
Message of Encouragement	
Face of Kindness	
Verse to Know	*Therefore encourage one another and build one another up, just as you are doing.* —1 Thessalonians 5:11 (ESV)
Resting Day?	
Fasting Day?	

Day 13

Time of Thankfulness	
Prayer for Others	
Act of Forgiveness	
Chapter to Read	Psalm 42
Hour of Generosity	
Message of Encouragement	
Face of Kindness	
Verse to Know	*There is one who speaks rashly, like a piercing sword; but the tongue of the wise brings healing.* —Proverbs 12:18 (HOL)
Resting Day?	
Fasting Day?	

Day 14

Time of Thankfulness	
Prayer for Others	
Act of Forgiveness	
Chapter to Read	Luke 11
Hour of Generosity	
Message of Encouragement	
Face of Kindness	
Verse to Know	*Oh give thanks to the LORD, for he is good, for his steadfast love endures forever!* —Psalm 107:1 (ESV)
Resting Day?	
Fasting Day?	

Day 15

Time of Thankfulness	
Prayer for Others	
Act of Forgiveness	
Chapter to Read	Psalm 51
Hour of Generosity	
Message of Encouragement	
Face of Kindness	
Verse to Know	*Enter His gates with thanksgiving and His courts with praise. Give thanks to Him and praise His name.* —Psalm 100:4 (HOL)
Resting Day?	
Fasting Day?	

Day 16

Time of Thankfulness	
Prayer for Others	
Act of Forgiveness	
Chapter to Read	Luke 17
Hour of Generosity	
Message of Encouragement	
Face of Kindness	
Verse to Know	*A joyful heart makes a cheerful face, but when the heart is sad, the spirit is broken.* —Proverbs 15:13 (NASB)
Resting Day?	
Fasting Day?	

Day 17

Time of Thankfulness	
Prayer for Others	
Act of Forgiveness	
Chapter to Read	James 4
Hour of Generosity	
Message of Encouragement	
Face of Kindness	
Verse to Know	*In the morning sow your seed, and at evening do not let your hand rest, because you don't know which will succeed, whether one or the other, or if both of them will be equally good.* —Ecclesiastes 11:6 (HOL)
Resting Day?	
Fasting Day?	

Day 18

Time of Thankfulness	
Prayer for Others	
Act of Forgiveness	
Chapter to Read	Romans 12
Hour of Generosity	
Message of Encouragement	
Face of Kindness	
Verse to Know	*Each one must give as he has decided in his heart, not reluctantly or under compulsion, for God loves a cheerful giver.* —2 Corinthians 9:7 (ESV)
Resting Day?	
Fasting Day?	

Day 19

Time of Thankfulness	
Prayer for Others	
Act of Forgiveness	
Chapter to Read	Ephesians 6
Hour of Generosity	
Message of Encouragement	
Face of Kindness	
Verse to Know	*But the fruit of the Spirit is love, joy, peace, patience, kindness, goodness, faithfulness, gentleness, self-control; against such things there is no law.* —Galatians 5:22–23 (NASB)
Resting Day?	
Fasting Day?	

Day 20

Time of Thankfulness	
Prayer for Others	
Act of Forgiveness	
Chapter to Read	Matthew 13
Hour of Generosity	
Message of Encouragement	
Face of Kindness	
Verse to Know	*Therefore confess your sins to each other and pray for each other so that you may be healed. The prayer of a righteous person is powerful and effective.* —James 5:16 (NIV)
Resting Day?	
Fasting Day?	

Day 21

Time of Thankfulness	
Prayer for Others	
Act of Forgiveness	
Chapter to Read	John 14
Hour of Generosity	
Message of Encouragement	
Face of Kindness	
Verse to Know	*Do not be anxious about anything, but in every situation, by prayer and petition, with thanksgiving, present your requests to God.* —Philippians 4:6 (NIV)
Resting Day?	
Fasting Day?	

Day 22

Time of Thankfulness	
Prayer for Others	
Act of Forgiveness	
Chapter to Read	Galatians 6
Hour of Generosity	
Message of Encouragement	
Face of Kindness	
Verse to Know	*Whenever you fast, do not put on a gloomy face as the hypocrites do, for they neglect their appearance so that they will be noticed by men when they are fasting. Truly I say to you, they have their reward in full.* —Matthew 6:16 (NASB)
Resting Day?	
Fasting Day?	

Day 23

Time of Thankfulness	
Prayer for Others	
Act of Forgiveness	
Chapter to Read	Psalm 91
Hour of Generosity	
Message of Encouragement	
Face of Kindness	
Verse to Know	*Give, and it will be given to you. A good measure, pressed down, shaken together, and running over will be poured into your lap. For with the measure you use, it will be measured back to you.* —Luke 6:38 (BSB)
Resting Day?	
Fasting Day?	

Day 24

Time of Thankfulness	
Prayer for Others	
Act of Forgiveness	
Chapter to Read	Matthew 18
Hour of Generosity	
Message of Encouragement	
Face of Kindness	
Verse to Know	*You will be made enriched in every way so that you can be generous on every occasion, and through us your generosity will result in thanksgiving to God.* —2 Corinthians 9:11 (NIV)
Resting Day?	
Fasting Day?	

Day 25

Time of Thankfulness	
Prayer for Others	
Act of Forgiveness	
Chapter to Read	John 15
Hour of Generosity	
Message of Encouragement	
Face of Kindness	
Verse to Know	*Jesus answered, "It is written: 'People do not live on bread alone, but on every word that comes from the mouth of God.'"* —Matthew 4:4 (NIV)
Resting Day?	
Fasting Day?	

Day 26

Time of Thankfulness	
Prayer for Others	
Act of Forgiveness	
Chapter to Read	1 John 2
Hour of Generosity	
Message of Encouragement	
Face of Kindness	
Verse to Know	*In the beginning was the Word, and the Word was with God, and the Word was God.* —John 1:1 (KJV)
Resting Day?	
Fasting Day?	

Day 27

Time of Thankfulness	
Prayer for Others	
Act of Forgiveness	
Chapter to Read	Psalm 100
Hour of Generosity	
Message of Encouragement	
Face of Kindness	
Verse to Know	*All Scripture is inspired by God and profitable for teaching, for reproof, for correction, for training in righteousness.* —2 Timothy 3:16 (NASB)
Resting Day?	
Fasting Day?	

Day 28

Time of Thankfulness	
Prayer for Others	
Act of Forgiveness	
Chapter to Read	Romans 8
Hour of Generosity	
Message of Encouragement	
Face of Kindness	
Verse to Know	*So shall my word be that goes out from my mouth; it shall not return to me empty, but it shall accomplish that which I purpose, and shall succeed in the thing for which I sent it.* —Isaiah 55:11 (ESV)
Resting Day?	
Fasting Day?	

Day 29

Time of Thankfulness	
Prayer for Others	
Act of Forgiveness	
Chapter to Read	Psalm 111
Hour of Generosity	
Message of Encouragement	
Face of Kindness	
Verse to Know	*Until now you have asked for nothing in My name. Ask and you will receive, so that your joy may be complete.* —John 16:24 (HOL)
Resting Day?	
Fasting Day?	

Day 30

Time of Thankfulness	
Prayer for Others	
Act of Forgiveness	
Chapter to Read	Colossians 3
Hour of Generosity	
Message of Encouragement	
Face of Kindness	
Verse to Know	*Therefore, as God's chosen people, holy and dearly loved, clothe yourselves with compassion, kindness, humility, gentleness and patience.* —Colossians 3:12 (NIV)
Resting Day?	
Fasting Day?	

Day 31

Time of Thankfulness	
Prayer for Others	
Act of Forgiveness	
Chapter to Read	Psalm 127
Hour of Generosity	
Message of Encouragement	
Face of Kindness	
Verse to Know	*For if you forgive other people when they sin against you, your heavenly Father will also forgive you.* —Matthew 6:14 (NIV)
Resting Day?	
Fasting Day?	

Day 32

Time of Thankfulness	
Prayer for Others	
Act of Forgiveness	
Chapter to Read	Ephesians 2
Hour of Generosity	
Message of Encouragement	
Face of Kindness	
Verse to Know	*The precepts of the LORD are right, rejoicing the heart; the commandment of the LORD is pure, enlightening the eyes.* —Psalm 19:8 (NASB)
Resting Day?	
Fasting Day?	

Day 33

Time of Thankfulness	
Prayer for Others	
Act of Forgiveness	
Chapter to Read	Psalm 139
Hour of Generosity	
Message of Encouragement	
Face of Kindness	
Verse to Know	*No discipline seems enjoyable at the time, but painful. Later on, however, it yields a peaceful harvest of righteousness to those who have been trained by it.* —Hebrews 12:11 (BSB)
Resting Day?	
Fasting Day?	

Day 34

Time of Thankfulness	
Prayer for Others	
Act of Forgiveness	
Chapter to Read	Ecclesiastes 2
Hour of Generosity	
Message of Encouragement	
Face of Kindness	
Verse to Know	*For the word of God is living and active, sharper than any two-edged sword, piercing to the division of soul and of spirit, of joints and of marrow, and discerning the thoughts and intentions of the heart.* —Hebrews 4:12 (ESV)
Resting Day?	
Fasting Day?	

Day 35

Time of Thankfulness	
Prayer for Others	
Act of Forgiveness	
Chapter to Read	Ephesians 6
Hour of Generosity	
Message of Encouragement	
Face of Kindness	
Verse to Know	*And Peter said to them, "Repent and be baptized every one of you in the name of Jesus Christ for the forgiveness of your sins, and you will receive the gift of the Holy Spirit.* —Acts 2:38 (ESV)
Resting Day?	
Fasting Day?	

Day 36

Time of Thankfulness	
Prayer for Others	
Act of Forgiveness	
Chapter to Read	James 1
Hour of Generosity	
Message of Encouragement	
Face of Kindness	
Verse to Know	*Tear your hearts, not just your clothes, and return to the LORD your God. For He is gracious and compassionate, slow to anger, rich in faithful love, and He relents from sending disaster.* —Joel 2:13 (HOL)
Resting Day?	
Fasting Day?	

Day 37

Time of Thankfulness	
Prayer for Others	
Act of Forgiveness	
Chapter to Read	Psalm 8
Hour of Generosity	
Message of Encouragement	
Face of Kindness	
Verse to Know	*And whatever you do, in word or deed, do everything in the name of the Lord Jesus, giving thanks to God the Father through him.* —Colossians 3:17 (ESV)
Resting Day?	
Fasting Day?	

Day 38

Time of Thankfulness	
Prayer for Others	
Act of Forgiveness	
Chapter to Read	1 John 3
Hour of Generosity	
Message of Encouragement	
Face of Kindness	
Verse to Know	*Cast your bread upon the waters, For you will find it after many days.* —Ecclesiastes 11:1 (NKJV)
Resting Day?	
Fasting Day?	

Day 39

Time of Thankfulness	
Prayer for Others	
Act of Forgiveness	
Chapter to Read	Psalm 20
Hour of Generosity	
Message of Encouragement	
Face of Kindness	
Verse to Know	*And he said to them, "Go into all the world and proclaim the gospel to the whole creation."* —Mark 16:15 (ESV)
Resting Day?	
Fasting Day?	

Day 40

Time of Thankfulness	
Prayer for Others	
Act of Forgiveness	
Chapter to Read	Revelation 22
Hour of Generosity	
Message of Encouragement	
Face of Kindness	
Verse to Know	*In everything give thanks: for this is the will of God in Christ Jesus concerning you.* —1 Thessalonians 5:18 (KJV)
Resting Day?	
Fasting Day?	

Destiny

You have finished! Congratulations on completing a forty-day feast for your soul.

Every dish was based on specific principles from the Bible. While these are powerful in their own right, a much deeper experience awaits those who accept God's gift of forgiveness by deciding to become a follower of Jesus.

Here are some key promises from the Bible about making that decision.

Jesus

Salvation is found in no one else, for there is no other name under heaven given to mankind by which we must be saved.
—Acts 4:12 (NIV)

Jesus said to him, "I am the way, and the truth, and the life. No one comes to the Father except through me."
—John 14:6 (ESV)

For God so loved the world, that he gave his only Son, that whoever believes in him should not perish but have eternal life.
—John 3:16 (ESV)

Becoming a Christian

If you confess with your mouth Jesus as Lord, and believe in your heart that God raised Him from the dead, you will be saved.
—Romans 10:9 (NASB)

And you will know the truth, and the truth will set you free.
—John 8:32 (ESV)

Christian Living

Then Jesus came to them and said,
"All authority in heaven and on earth has been given to me.
Therefore go and make disciples of all nations, baptizing them
in the name of the Father and of the Son and of the Holy Spirit,
and teaching them to obey everything I have commanded you.
And surely I am with you always, to the very end of the age."
—Matthew 28:18–20 (NIV)

For the whole law is fulfilled in one word:
"You shall love your neighbor as yourself."
... the fruit of the Spirit is love, joy, peace, patience,
kindness, goodness, faithfulness, gentleness, self-control;
against such things there is no law.
—Galatians 5:14, 22–23 (ESV)

Do not be anxious, saying, 'What shall we eat?' or 'What shall
we drink?' or 'What shall we wear?' For the Gentiles seek
after all these things, and your heavenly Father knows that
you need them all. But seek first the kingdom of God and his
righteousness, and all these things will be added to you.
—Matthew 6:31–32 (ESV)

Now to him who is able to do immeasurably more than all
we ask or imagine, according to his power that is at work
within us, to him be glory in the church and in Christ Jesus
throughout all generations, for ever and ever! Amen.
—Ephesians 3:20–21 (NIV)

Right now you have the opportunity to experience the freedom that comes from following Jesus Christ. His sacrifice of dying on the cross is full payment to release you and heal you from everything in your past, and His spirit will guide you into a future with eternal value.

Declare aloud that "Jesus is Lord" and be born again as a child of God, a prince or princess in his kingdom with supernatural power and an inheritance that lasts forever.

Congratulations and welcome. You will never be the same again.

My Story

Jesus has done some amazing things in my life. At a very young age, I remember feeling angry that anyone could be stupid enough to believe in God. I don't know where that came from. Not my parents, who described themselves as agnostic, sympathetic to faith but unable to find it for themselves.

At some point, though, the idea of a loving God started to grow, perhaps through the prayers and stories of my kindergarten teachers. They used to pray with their classes, and in hindsight I realize that the songs we learned to sing were from church. Thank you ladies.

One time I remember a family holiday with a six-hour car journey into the country when I was six years old. We stopped for water at a little village church and I still remember the Bible verse inscribed above the garden tap:

> *Whosoever drinketh of this water shall thirst again:*
> *But whosoever drinketh of the water that I shall give him*
> *shall never thirst.*
> —John 4:13 (KJV)

The verse made no sense and intrigued me so much that it stayed with me to this day. Scripture has unique power to stick in our minds and surface when needed. I'm passionate about getting scriptures into our communities using every means available, and this book is born from that passion.

One day, my dad returned from a work trip to America with a special edition Bible called *The Highest Flight,* which celebrated

American exploits in space.[5] For some reason, I didn't doubt the truth of those scriptures, but nor did I understand their meaning or what they meant for my life. Years later, I would take that Bible to my church youth group, and none of the verses ever matched anyone else's translation!

A classmate in high school, Crawford, turned around during a science practical and straight up asked me if I believed in Jesus. My noncommittal answer prompted Crawford to assert:

> "You can't sit on the fence. You have to make a decision to follow Jesus if you want to be saved."

I knew he was right. There is a sense of conviction that comes with spiritual truths that defies logic and reason. These truths are one of the things that make the Bible so compelling to believers. Its verses contain layers of meaning that continually reveal new insights regardless of whether you are just casually browsing or a scholar with decades of research.

It doesn't bother me that some verses are contradictory. Proverbs 26:4–5 is a great example of that:

> *Answer not a fool according to his folly,*
> *lest thou also be like unto him.*
> *Answer a fool according to his folly,*
> *lest he be wise in his own conceit.*
> —Proverbs 26:4–5 (KJV)

---

[5] Following his flight to the moon on *Apollo 15*, astronaut James (Jim) B. Irwin devoted his life to Christian evangelism. Part of his outreach was a project to relate scripture to his adventure in the space program. *The Highest Flight* was an illustrated edition of The Living New Testament (A New Testament paraphrase by Ken Taylor) published for the High Flight Foundation by World Home Bible League in 1971.

Obviously, verses like these provide leeway to use our own judgment based on circumstances. The whole point of scripture is that the words are living and active[6]. As we read them, the Holy Spirit "guides us into all truth.[7]" Some times I've read verses out of context that are so perfectly timed and relevant that they are surely a divine nudge.

Half the battle is remembering to seek God's will rather than our own. When we're listening and responsive to divine promptings, then we can make decisions and take actions with great confidence. Even when we make mistakes, I am convinced God causes wrong decisions to work out for our good[8].

So back to the story. Sometime after Crawford's challenge, another school friend, Mark, invited me to the evening youth service at his Anglican church. I was thirteen. Mark was hugely charismatic and seemed to get on with everyone. I agreed to go.

The first Sunday, I walked for two kilometers to what I thought was his church. The main building was locked, but I could see people already gathered in a hall at the back. They were standing in a circle, holding hands, and singing. Then they would all go in to the center and huddle around each other, holding out their hands or embracing each other. I couldn't see Mark and was shocked at the intimacy between all those people. I reasoned they must all be from the same family because I had never seen non-relatives being so affectionate with one another! It was weird.

I described my experience to Mark next day at school and realized I had been at the wrong church! Next Sunday, I found Mark's church and as a young teenager quickly learned to appreciate the warmth of Christian fellowship. I also learned

---

[6] Hebrews 4:12

[7] John 6:45, Acts 8:32

[8] Romans 8:28

about the difference between living for ourselves and choosing to live for God, about laying down our lives and asking Jesus to be Lord, about repenting for sin and being forgiven, about discerning God's voice and direction, and about praying for miracles and seeing them happen. I even upgraded to a leather-bound NIV Bible.

During those years, we used to go to an annual Christian music festival called Black Stump, and I'll never forget one of the keynote speakers, John Smith. This old man had left his parish ministry and went to live in a bikie community, creating a ministry called the God Squad. They dressed in their leather and chains and rode Harleys up and down Australia's outback roads praying for and ministering to anyone in need. John Smith was my first hero of the Christian faith.

One thing we didn't learn at my church was how to have healthy relationships or a godly perspective on marriage. It seemed everyone was going out with someone, even the leaders. It wasn't until many years later that I experienced a youth culture that was truly sold out for God. More on that later.

When we graduated from high school everyone went their separate ways, mostly to university or to travel. I joined an exchange program and prepared to live with a host family and attend high school in Japan. The depth of relationship between my new AFS friends seemed much greater than I had experienced in church fellowship. We spent months together preparing for our trips overseas, and I became disillusioned with church. My church friends had stopped going, there were no programs for school leavers, and I had quickly developed much deeper friendships with my new mostly non-Christian exchange-student friends.

This was the start of a number of years in a kind of wilderness. I knew God but was caught up in study and work. I was living a basically secular life with Christian morals, the worst of both worlds. When I did visit churches, I found them distant and boring. I travelled to the UK to explore my English heritage and stayed, first for postgraduate study in Edinburgh and then because I was recruited by an international consulting firm. Once again, I had a new tribe, and I embraced the richness of experience that wealthy Brits take for granted.

It was during this season that God made a dramatic reappearance in my life.

The consulting firm was relocating me from London to Manchester, and I was finishing up an assignment for a Czech company. I was sitting in my room in the firm's apartment in Prague, and my leather-bound study Bible, which I still carried when I travelled, was on the bed. It had fallen open to 1 Samuel and described Eli rebuking his sons.

Eli's words struck me to my core. Like Eli's sons, I, too, was guilty. I, too, had sinned against God's servants. I, too, was ignoring His rebuke and was literally going to die. After years of only halfheartedly acknowledging my dormant faith, I experienced an overwhelming sense of guilt and shame at the way I had been treating God and His people.

I knelt next to that bed, confessed all the wrong things I had been doing, and experienced the amazing release that comes when you receive God's forgiveness. Even though we can't see it, the Bible describes how God literally washes away our guilt and shame with Jesus's blood. This divine act of grace is the essence of the Bible narrative and the Christian faith.

Still slightly dazed from my encounter with forgiveness, I walked downstairs and, to my surprise, heard voices singing a familiar church song. The door to the meeting room was open, so I entered to find an American missionary leading a worship service for local believers. In all of Prague, an English-speaking church group had been worshiping right under my feet when God called me to rededicate my life. We prayed together and met several more times in the two weeks before my assignment ended. I headed to Manchester to find an apartment and start life in a new city.

At first, I lived in temporary accommodation in Manchester City. The next work assignment was for a logistics company based in Bedfordshire, about four hours' drive from Manchester and an hour from London. I needed a church to call home, but it's difficult to plug in to a church community when you are travelling all the time. My previous attempts to find a church had been thwarted by constantly moving around and needing valuable weekend time to simply catch up on basic chores.

Back in Australia, my favorite youth leaders had been influenced by John Wimber and his Vineyard movement, so I decided to try Manchester's one and only Vineyard church. It was a congregation of all ages and, as I recall, fairly full. I sat down next to a lad about my age, and he quickly introduced himself as James.

As I look back on my life today, meeting James was both miraculous and a pivotal moment.

It transpired that James was one of the few people in church with a job like mine (we were called yuppies back then) and, critically, that his brother was both a committed believer and living in Bedford, right where I would be spending my weekdays for the next six months. In fact, meeting James connected me with a group of faithful young men and women spread between London, Bedford, and Manchester. Before long, I was sharing a flat with James and another friend Paul.

For the first time in my life, I experienced fellowship with Christian brothers and sisters who were truly counter cultural, genuinely aspiring to live lives that aligned with biblical principles in every area. I was warmly embraced by the Bedford congregation, starting with James's brother Pete and his friends.

The young pastor, twenty-one-year-old Matt Hatch, with wisdom and maturity beyond his age, had created an amazing youth culture that was literally transforming the city. High school students growing up in the church couldn't wait to take a voluntary gap year and serve in the homeless shelter they had established. What a contrast to the "convenient Christianity" I had lived until then!

Not long after meeting James and becoming part of the London-Bedford-Manchester group, I had my next life-changing experience. A group of young women organized regular social events to bring everyone together, and James, Paul, and I were all heading into the Lake District for three days of camping and hiking.

The three of us had an instant connection with one particular girl on the trip. She seemed so natural and unaffected, completely at home in the outdoors, affectionate, tactile, caring, and comfortable with everyone. She was unselfconscious and unafraid. Her name was Claire.

We were all three smitten with Claire. We found out that she had grown up in Zimbabwe during the bush war, studied nursing in South Africa, and trained in the townships of the Cape Flats, pulling knives and spears from rival gang members sometimes still fighting in the emergency rooms.

It was my luck after the trip to be closest to London where Claire was now working. She stayed in nurses' accommodation and worked in intensive care at a private hospital for officers. I was soon making the trip from Bedford regularly to visit Claire and her friends.

As our friendship blossomed, we agreed (or she let me know, I don't recall exactly) that if we were serious, there would be a ring on her finger within a year and a wedding within two. I travelled to Zimbabwe to meet her parents, Anne and John, on their commercial farm. John grew the specialized seed for seed cotton, and the Glendale farmers built and maintained an orphanage and clinic for the local community in the absence of reliable public infrastructure. Anne and John were incredibly generous hosts, as was the entire farming community (who all wanted to meet me), and I had no inkling of their strong reservations about the distance between Australia and Zimbabwe.

I moved to London and joined Claire's church, called His People. She had been one of the first members when it was founded by Pastor Paul Daniels on the campuses of Cape Town and still remembers serving tea and coffee to a congregation of less than thirty. By the time Pastors Wolfgang and Alison Eckleben came to start a church in London, there were congregations at campuses all over South Africa. The London church was a home for students travelling from South Africa on working visas and many local students as well.

His People established a Bible school that ran on the campuses during weeknights. Running for two years, the Bible school course provided a solid theological foundation that every Christian could benefit from. Until then, I had always been envious of people who had the opportunity to study formal theology.

I asked Claire to marry me within the agreed time frame, and we had the wedding a few months later. Our pastors travelled all the way to Zimbabwe to officiate the ceremony, which took place in the grounds of a beautiful private game reserve. Claire arrived on the back of an elephant, and a female impala gave birth the same day. We felt incredibly blessed.

In London, Claire started working in the church office and took over administration of the Bible school. Together we became de facto parents for many of the young people so far away from home, and our network of small groups spread across East London. Some weeks, we would make the long round-trip from our apartment in the east to the West Kensington church every single day.

One time, the traffic was so bad we completely missed the first service and just made it in time for the second. Another time, we were running impossibly late, yet every single light on the route was green, saving half an hour and allowing us to arrive early. It was so miraculous that by the end I wasn't even slowing for red lights, knowing they would be green by the time I reached them. And every one was. Either God performed a miracle, or someone was using us to test out a new traffic management system!

During this time, His People church joined with Every Nation, another campus-based church with congregations in America and Asia. We had the privilege of getting to know the leaders of the new movement and ended up relocating to the Philippines to found a software company and serve the church there.

The founding pastor, Steve Murrell, first travelled to the Philippines on a two-month mission trip. By the time we were there, twenty years had elapsed, and he was still faithfully ministering to the Philippines with his wife, Nancy.

Many of the students whom Steve had ministered to on campus now had prominent roles in business, government, and the arts. One unforgettable church conference coincided with a sold-out concert by Asia's version of Justin Bieber. As the worship ended, this superstar came onto the stage, all dressed for his main concert next door, and led another set of worship. Honestly, the roof came off that place. Pastor Steve's team had been leading that young man in the faith since well before his big break.

One of the things Steve did really well was raising up new leaders. I think this is a key differentiator between churches that get stuck around a few hundred people and those that turn into movements and spread across a region or country. The head pastor must be able to raise up new leaders and give them freedom to lead.

Joey Bonifacio was one of those leaders. I will never forget Joey's comment, with no hint of pride or self-aggrandizement, that after decades of faithfully serving God, there really wasn't much sin left to deal with. I had never heard someone speak like that, but knowing Joey and his family personally I realize victory over sin is possible. Truly inspiring.

Since then, I sold my software business and returned to Australia so that our children, who were born in England, the Philippines, and Australia, could grow up knowing their extended family, something I never foresaw as we established ourselves in the UK.

Claire's parents, John and Anne, had their farm taken by the Zimbabwe state without compensation and saw their life savings evaporate in the furnace of hyperinflation. They now stay with us (how things change) still navigating byzantine rules of residence after nearly a decade.

The Bible ministry I founded, TopVerses.com, which was inspired in the Philippines but came to life in just a couple of weekends in Australia, is now ten years old and receives thousands of daily visitors. The internet is surely God's gift for us to reach every corner of the world with His Word.

One of TopVerses' initiatives, in conjunction with other Bible ministries, has been to place Bible verses on web pages around the world using Google Ads technology. Some of the greatest click-through rates have come from the least hospitable places you could imagine.

Most of all, I am passionate about the role the church should play in technology innovation. We should be leading the world, just as we used to lead in music, art, architecture, education, science, and many other disciplines.

In conclusion, this book is an act of faith. I feel so grateful for this opportunity to put scriptures in front of people and I know it will change lives, including yours if you allow. The word of God is alive and active – it judges your thoughts and the attitude of your heart.[9]

My first encounter with the spiritual disciplines came as a teenager through a book called *Celebration of Discipline* by Richard Foster. I highly recommend it for anyone looking to go deeper into the topic.

Finally, while I realize that *The Forty-Day Feast* just scratches the surface of these profound disciplines, I'm trusting that even the tiniest mustard seed can grow into something extraordinary when God blesses it. May this be so for you.

Yours in Christ,

Pete

---

[9] Hebrews 4:12

Printed in the United States
By Bookmasters